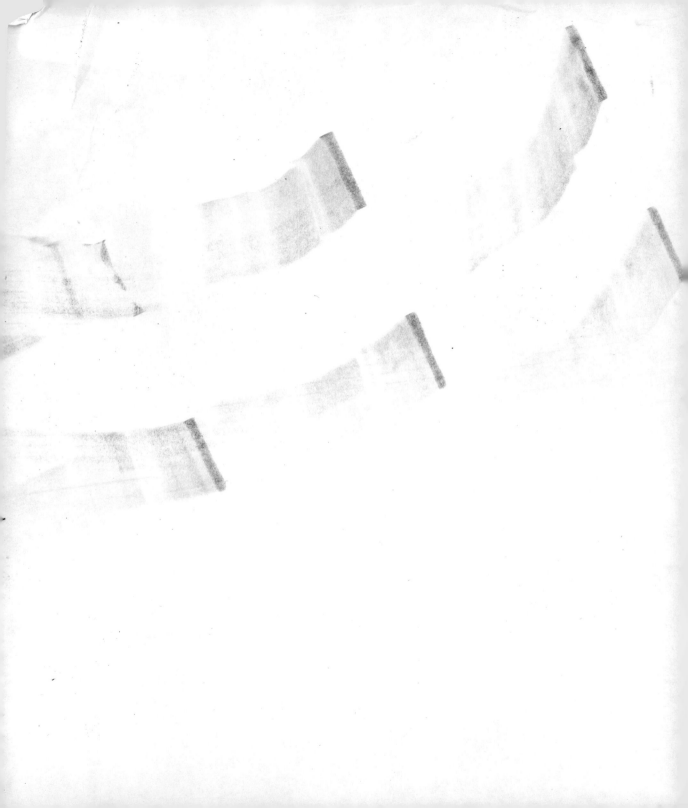

Animal Babies

Reptiles

Rod Theodorou

Heinemann Library
Chicago, Illinois

© 2000 Reed Educational & Professional Publishing
Published by Heinemann Library,
an imprint of Reed Educational & Professional Publishing,
Chicago, IL

Customer Service 1-888-454-2279
Visit our website at www.heinemannlibrary.com

Text designed by Celia Floyd
Illustrations by Alan Fraser
Printed in Hong Kong/China

04
10 9 8 7 6 5 4

The Library of Congress has cataloged the hardcover version of this book as follows:
Library of Congress Cataloging-in-Publication Data
Theodorou, Rod.
    Reptiles / Rod Theodorou.
        p. cm. -- (Animal babies)
    Includes bibliographical references and index.
    Summary: Introduces the birth, development, care, feeding, and
characteristics of baby reptiles.
        ISBN 1-57572-884-2 (lib.bdg.)
    1. Reptiles—Infancy—Juvenile literature. 2. Parental behavior
in animals—Juvenile literature. [1. Reptiles. 2. Animals—
Infancy. 3. Parental behavior in animals.] I. Title.
    II. Series: Animal babies (Des Plaines, Ill.)
QL644.2.T48 1999
597.9'139—dc21   99-18054
                                                      CIP
Paperback ISBN 1-57572-545-2

Acknowledgments
The Publishers would like to thank the following for permission to reproduce photographs:

BBC/Michael Pitts, p. 6; Martha Holmes, p. 7; Tony Pooley, p. 14; Pete Oxford, p. 16; Mike Wilkes, p. 26; Bruce Coleman/Jane Burton, p. 20; Frank Lane/T. Davidson, p. 8; J. Louwman, p. 18; NHPA/Daniel Heuclin, p. 10; Karl Switak, p. 12; B. Jones & M. Shimlock, p. 17; Rich Kirchner, p. 23; Eric Soder, p. 25; OSF/Michael & Patricia Fogden, p. 5; Mark Jones, p. 9; Maurice Tibbles, p. 11; Martin Chillmaid, p. 15; Z. Leszczynski, pp. 21, 24; M. Deeble & V. Stone, p. 22; Dr. F. Koster, p. 27; Tony Stone/Stephen Cooper, p. 13; Gary Braasch, p. 19.

Cover photo: Animals Animals/Zig Leszczynski

Some words in this book are in bold, **like this.** You can find out what they mean by looking in the glossary.

Contents

Introduction

There are many different kinds of animals. All animals have babies. They take care of their babies in different ways.

These are the six main animal groups.

Mammal   Bird   Reptile

Amphibian   Fish   Insect

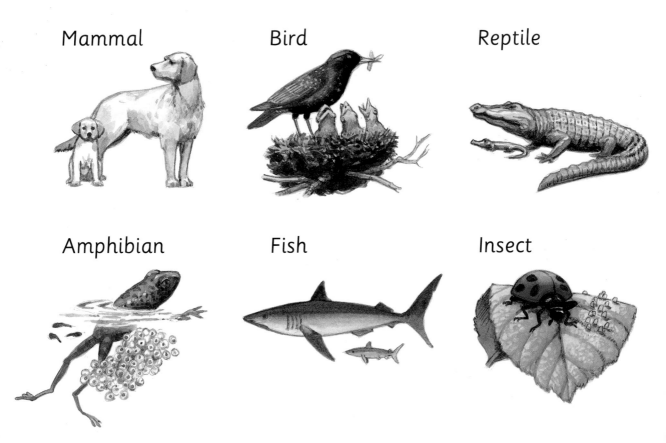

This book is about reptiles. Lizards, snakes, crocodiles, alligators, tortoises, and turtles are all reptiles. Reptiles live in most parts of the world except the very cold places.

This Australian bearded lizard lives in the desert.

What Is a Reptile?

All reptiles:
- breathe air
- are covered in **scaly** skin

Komodo dragon

Scaly skin

Most reptiles:

- **hatch** from eggs females **lay** on land
- are colored to match their surroundings
- have to move back and forth between sun and shade to keep warm or cool down

This marine iguana sunbathes for most of the day.

Building a Nest

Female reptiles **lay** their eggs in holes in the ground or under rocks. Alligators make huge nests out of mud and leaves.

Alligators dig a hole in the middle of their nests, where they lay their eggs.

Sea turtles spend all their lives in the water, but they lay their eggs on land. During the night they crawl to a beach and dig a deep hole in the sand, where they lay their eggs.

This turtle uses its **flippers** to dig a hole.

Laying Eggs

Most reptile eggs are white and soft like paper or **leather**. They are full of **yolk**, just like a bird's egg.

Some lizards and snakes, like this boa constrictor, do not **lay** eggs. Their babies are born alive.

Many reptile babies are eaten by **predators**, so female reptiles lay lots and lots of eggs. This way some of their babies will live to be adults.

This female green turtle can lay up to two hundred eggs in one night!

Taking Care of the Eggs

Most reptiles **lay** their eggs and then leave them. They do not look after them or **protect** the **hatchlings**. A few reptiles do stay with their eggs.

This python is one of the few reptiles that stays with its eggs. It has wrapped itself around the eggs to keep them warm.

Alligators take good care of their nests and eggs. The mother stands by the nest. She will not eat for weeks just so she can stay with her eggs.

Alligators will attack any **predators** who want to steal their eggs.

Hatching Eggs

When some baby alligators or crocodiles are ready to **hatch,** they start to make grunting sounds inside the egg. The mother hears them and scratches open the nest to help them escape.

This crocodile mother is carefully cracking open an egg with her jaws to help the baby escape.

Baby snakes and crocodiles have a special sharp bump called an egg-tooth on their **snouts**. This helps them cut or crack open their egg.

After hatching, these baby corn snakes may rest in their broken eggs for hours before they slide off.

Race for Life

Once female turtles have buried their eggs in a hole, they go back to the water. About six weeks later, the eggs **hatch**. Crabs and seabirds gather on the beach to eat the babies.

These turtle **hatchlings** have to dig their way up through the sand in their nest.

The tiny hatchlings have to crawl as fast as they can to the sea. Even in the sea there may be large fish and hungry sharks waiting to eat them.

Only a few turtles **survive** to become adults.

Live Birth

Some reptiles do not **lay** eggs. Their babies grow inside them and then are born live.

Some kinds of chameleons lay eggs, but others give birth to live young.

When the babies are born, their mother does not take care of them. The babies leave their mother and start to look for food.

This huge anaconda snake can give birth to up to 50 live babies at a time. Each baby is as long as your arm!

Finding Food

Reptile parents do not feed their **hatchlings**. The moment reptiles are born they have to catch their own food. They eat insects and other small animals.

This young crocodile has to catch its own fish.

Reptile babies are born strong and fast. They can hunt for food just like their parents.

This baby copperhead snake's tail looks like a tasty worm. When an animal tries to eat it, the snake bites and eats the animal.

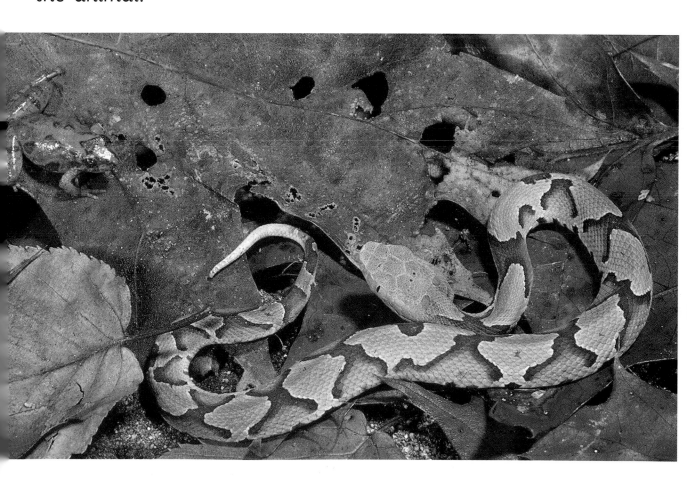

Taking Care of Baby

Crocodiles and alligators do take good care of their babies. The babies stay together in groups. The adults watch out for **predators**, like snakes or birds.

Sometimes Nile crocodile mothers carry their babies on their back to keep them safe.

Alligator babies call out to their parents when they need help. If one of them gets lost, it will make a loud call. The large females quickly rush to find it.

Mother alligators take care of their babies for up to three years.

Staying Safe

Baby reptiles are very small. Many other animals hunt and eat them. Most reptiles stay safe by keeping very still, so they are hard to spot, or by quickly running away.

This baby chameleon is smaller than your little finger.

Baby lizards can drop their tails if they need to. If a **predator** grabs a lizard by its tail, the tail drops off and keeps flopping around. While the predator is busy with the tail, the lizard can run away.

This common wall lizard will slowly grow a new tail.

Growing Up

As many reptiles grow, they get too big for their skin. Their skin splits and comes off, leaving new skin underneath. This is called **shedding**.

This grass snake's old skin has come off in long strips.

Some reptiles grow quickly. By the time they are one year old, crocodiles are almost as long as your arm. Newborn tortoises are tiny and grow much more slowly.

A newborn tortoise is not much bigger than your fist.

Reptiles and Other Animals

		Fish
What they look like:	Bones inside body	all
	Number of legs	none
	Hair on body	none
	Scaly skin	most
	Wings	none
	Feathers	none
Where they live:	Live on land	none
	Live in water	all
How they are born:	Grow babies inside body	some
	Hatch from eggs	most
How babies get food:	Get milk from mother	none
	Parents bring food	none

Amphibians	Insects	Reptiles	Birds	Mammals
all	none	all	all	all
4 or none	6	4 or none	2	2 or 4
none	all	none	none	all
none	none	all	none	few
none	most	none	all	some
none	none	none	all	none
most	most	most	all	most
some	some	some	none	some
few	some	some	none	most
most	most	most	all	few
none	none	none	none	all
none	none	none	most	most

Glossary

flipper flat part of a reptile's body that sticks out and is used for swimming

hatch to be born from an egg

hatchling name for a baby when it has just been born from an egg

lay when an egg comes out of a female reptile's body

leather animal skin that is used to make shoes, clothes, or bags

predator animal that hunts and kills other animals for food

protect to keep safe

scaly covered with small, flat pieces of hard, dry skin

shed to lose an old layer of skin when a new, bigger one has grown

snout long nose

survive to stay alive

yolk part of an egg that is food for a baby animal

More Books to Read

Butterfield, Moira. *Fierce, Strong, & Snappy.* Austin, Tex.: Raintree Steck-Vaughn Publishers, 1998.

Crewe, Sabrina. *The Alligator.* Austin, Tex.: Raintree Steck-Vaughn Publishers, 1998.

Gish, Melissa. *Snakes.* Mankato, Minn.: The Creative Company, 1998.

Hansen, Ann L. *Turtles.* Edina, Minn.: ABDO Publishing Company, 1997.

Robinson, Claire. *Crocodile.* Crystal Lake, Ill.: Heinemann Library, 1997.

—. *Snakes.* Des Plaines, Ill.: Heinemann Library, 1999.

Schlaepfer, Gloria G., and Mary L. Samuelson. *Pythons & Boas.* Parsippany, N.J.: Silver Burdett Press, 1999.

Index